Promoting Accessibility in Technology Education for Students with Disabilities

By

Umar Ibrahim

©

2024

Table Of Contents

1. Title: 1
2. Table of Contents: 2
3. Abstract: 5
4. Chapter 1: Introduction: 6
5. Chapter 2: Understanding Accessibility in Technology Education: 9
6. Chapter 3: Challenges Faced by Students with Disabilities: 13
7. Chapter 4: Importance of Promoting Accessibility: 17
8. Chapter 5: Strategies for Promoting Accessibility: 20
9. Chapter 6: Assistive Technologies in Technology Education: 24
10. Chapter 7: Inclusive Curriculum Design: 29
11. Chapter 8: Collaboration with Special Education Professionals: 33
12. Chapter 9: Training and Professional Development for Teachers: 36
13. Chapter 10: Creating Accessible Digital Content: 40
14. Chapter 11: Universal Design Principles in Technology Education: 43
15. Chapter 12: Providing Accommodations and Modifications: 46

16. Chapter 13: Ensuring Physical Accessibility in Technology Classrooms: 50

17. Chapter 14: Addressing Attitudes and Stereotypes: 54

18. Chapter 15: Promoting Inclusive Classroom Culture: 58

19. Chapter 16: Supporting Social and Emotional Well-being: 63

20. Chapter 17: Parent and Family Engagement: 67

21. Chapter 18: Advocacy for Accessibility in Technology Education: 71

22. Chapter 19: Evaluating and Assessing Accessibility: 75

23. Chapter 20: Funding and Resources for Accessibility Initiatives: 79

24. Chapter 21: Case Studies: Successful Implementation of Accessibility: 83

25. Chapter 22: Promoting Accessibility in Online Learning Environments: 87

26. Chapter 23: Collaborating with Industry and Technology Companies: 92

27. Chapter 24: Promoting Career Opportunities for Students with Disabilities: 96

28. Chapter 25: Ensuring Equitable Access to Extracurricular Technology Activities: 100

29. Chapter 26: Promoting Accessibility in STEM Education: 104

30. Chapter 27: Addressing Intersectionality in Accessibility Initiatives: 109

31. Chapter 28: Legislation and Policies for Accessibility in Education: 110

32. Chapter 29: Building Partnerships with Disability Organizations: 113

33. Chapter 30: Research and Evidence-based Practices: 116

34. Chapter 31: Continuous Improvement and Reflection: 120

35. Conclusion: 123

ABSTRACT

In today's digital age, access to technology education is imperative. However, students with disabilities often encounter substantial barriers in accessing technology-based learning resources and tools. This research paper aims to examine the current state of accessibility in technology education for students with disabilities, shedding light on the challenges and opportunities in this critical area. Through a comprehensive literature review and empirical investigation, this study identifies key barriers and recommends strategies to promote accessibility. The findings emphasize the importance of adopting inclusive approaches, leveraging assistive technology, and adhering to accessibility guidelines to ensure equitable and accessible technology education for all students, regardless of their abilities. This research contributes to the ongoing discourse on inclusive education and underscores the urgency of addressing accessibility concerns in technology education for students with disabilities to foster a more inclusive and equitable learning environment.

Chapter 1

INTRODUCTION:

In the vast landscape of education, the transformative power of technology is undeniable. It has revolutionized how we learn, communicate, and interact with the world around us. From online resources to interactive software, technology has become an integral part of modern education, promising boundless opportunities for students to explore, create, and innovate.

However, amid this digital revolution, there exists a significant challenge – ensuring that technology is accessible to all learners, including those with disabilities. For students with disabilities, accessing and engaging with technology can be fraught with obstacles, ranging from physical barriers to attitudinal biases. Despite the strides made in educational inclusion, there remains a pressing need to bridge the accessibility gap in technology education.

This book, "Promoting Accessibility in Technology Education for Students with Disabilities," serves as a guiding light in navigating this complex terrain. It is a comprehensive exploration of the multifaceted dimensions of accessibility in technology education, offering insights, strategies, and best practices for creating inclusive learning environments where every student can thrive.

At its core, this book advocates for equity – the principle that every student, regardless of ability, deserves equal access to educational opportunities. Equity in education is not merely a moral imperative; it is a legal mandate enshrined in legislation such as the Individuals with Disabilities Education Act (IDEA) and the Americans with Disabilities Act (ADA). Yet, achieving true equity requires more than just compliance with laws and regulations; it demands a proactive commitment to dismantling barriers and fostering a culture of inclusivity.

The journey towards accessibility in technology education is multifaceted, encompassing various aspects of curriculum design, instructional practices, and institutional policies. It requires a holistic approach that recognizes the unique needs and strengths of students with disabilities and empowers educators to address these needs effectively.

Throughout this book, readers will embark on a transformative journey, exploring topics ranging from the fundamentals of accessibility to practical strategies for implementation. Each chapter delves into a specific aspect of promoting accessibility in technology education, offering actionable insights backed by research and real-world examples.

From understanding the challenges faced by students with disabilities to advocating for policy changes, this book provides a roadmap for educators, administrators, policymakers, and other stakeholders committed to creating inclusive learning environments. It emphasizes the importance of collaboration, innovation, and continuous improvement in advancing accessibility initiatives and ensuring that every student has the opportunity to reach their full potential.

As we embark on this journey together, let us reaffirm our commitment to the fundamental principle that education is a universal right – a right that must be accessible to all, regardless of ability. By promoting accessibility in technology education, we not only level the playing field for students with disabilities but also enrich the educational experience for all learners, fostering a more inclusive and equitable society.

Chapter 2

UNDERSTANDING ACCESSIBILITY IN TECHNOLOGY EDUCATION

Accessibility: Accessibility in technology education refers to the design and implementation of educational resources, tools, and environments that can be accessed and effectively used by all students, including those with disabilities. It encompasses various aspects, including physical accessibility, cognitive accessibility, and socio-emotional accessibility.

Legal Framework: Accessibility in education is not just a matter of best practice; it is often a legal requirement. Laws such as the Americans with Disabilities Act (ADA) in the United States and similar legislation in other countries mandate equal access to education for students with disabilities. These laws provide a framework for ensuring that educational institutions accommodate the needs of all students, regardless of their abilities.

Types of Disabilities: Accessibility in technology education encompasses a wide range of disabilities, including but not limited to:

- ✓ Physical disabilities: Mobility impairments, fine motor skill impairments, and sensory impairments (visual, auditory, etc.).

- ✓ Cognitive disabilities: Learning disabilities, attention disorders, and intellectual disabilities.

- Neurodiversity: Autism spectrum disorders, ADHD, and other neurological differences.
- Invisible disabilities: Chronic health conditions, mental health disorders, and other conditions that may not be immediately apparent but can impact learning.

Barriers to Accessibility: There are various barriers that students with disabilities may encounter in technology education, including:

- Physical barriers: Inaccessible buildings, classrooms, and technology tools.
- Technological barriers: Software and hardware that are not designed with accessibility features, such as screen readers or alternative input methods.
- Attitudinal barriers: Negative attitudes, stereotypes, and misconceptions about disabilities that can create a hostile or unwelcoming environment for students.
- Financial barriers: Lack of funding for assistive technology devices or accommodations.

Universal Design for Learning (UDL): Universal Design for Learning is an approach to curriculum design that aims to make learning accessible to all students from the outset. It emphasizes providing multiple means of representation, engagement, and expression to accommodate diverse learner needs. UDL principles can be applied to technology education to ensure that instructional materials and activities are accessible to students with disabilities.

Accessible Technology Tools: Advances in technology have led to the development of a wide range of accessible tools and software applications that can support students with disabilities in their learning. These include:

- Screen readers: Software programs that convert text into speech or braille, making digital content accessible to students with visual impairments.

- Speech recognition software: Tools that allow students to dictate text or control computer applications using their voice, benefiting students with mobility impairments or learning disabilities.

- Alternative input devices: Devices such as joysticks, trackballs, or switches that provide alternative methods of input for students who may have difficulty using a standard keyboard or mouse.

Inclusive Design Principles: In addition to UDL, inclusive design principles focus on designing products, environments, and experiences that are usable by the widest possible range of people, regardless of their abilities. In technology education, inclusive design principles can guide the development of accessible websites, applications, and digital content.

Collaboration and Partnerships: Promoting accessibility in technology education requires collaboration and partnerships between various stakeholders, including educators, administrators, parents, disability advocates, and technology companies. By working together, these stakeholders can identify barriers to accessibility and develop solutions that meet the diverse needs of students with disabilities.

Chapter 3

CHALLENGES FACED BY STUDENTS WITH DISABILITIES

Students with disabilities encounter a myriad of challenges in accessing and participating in technology education. Understanding these challenges is crucial for developing effective strategies to promote accessibility and inclusion. This chapter explores various challenges faced by students with disabilities in technology education:

Physical Barriers: Physical disabilities such as mobility impairments can present significant barriers to accessing technology education. Students with mobility impairments may encounter difficulties navigating physical spaces, reaching equipment, or participating in hands-on activities. Lack of wheelchair-accessible facilities, inaccessible furniture arrangements, and limited availability of adaptive technology further exacerbate these challenges.

Digital Accessibility: Digital accessibility remains a major challenge for students with disabilities in technology education. Many educational resources, including online platforms, software applications, and digital content, are not designed with accessibility features in mind. This poses barriers to students with visual impairments, hearing impairments, and other disabilities, hindering their ability to fully engage with instructional materials and activities.

Attitudinal Barriers: Attitudinal barriers, including stereotypes, stigma, and discrimination, contribute to the marginalization of students with disabilities in technology education. Negative attitudes and misconceptions about disability may lead to low expectations, limited opportunities, and social exclusion. These attitudes can influence the behaviour of educators, peers, and even the students themselves, creating a hostile or unwelcoming learning environment.

Lack of Support and Accommodations: Many students with disabilities face challenges in accessing the support and accommodations they need to succeed in technology education. Limited availability of assistive technology, specialized instruction, and individualized support services can hinder their academic progress and independence. Inadequate funding, resource constraints, and bureaucratic barriers further exacerbate these challenges, leaving students with disabilities underserved and marginalized.

Curriculum Accessibility: The lack of accessible curriculum materials and instructional methods presents significant barriers to learning for students with disabilities. Traditional teaching approaches may not adequately address the diverse learning needs and preferences of students with disabilities, leading to gaps in understanding, engagement, and achievement. Moreover, inaccessible curriculum content, including text-heavy materials, complex graphics, and multimedia presentations, may impede access to information and hinder comprehension for students with certain disabilities.

Social and Emotional Challenges: Students with disabilities often face social and emotional challenges that impact their participation and engagement in technology education. Bullying, peer rejection, and feelings of isolation can undermine their confidence, self-esteem, and sense of belonging in the classroom. Moreover, the stigma associated with disability may contribute to anxiety, depression, and other mental health issues, further complicating their educational experience.

Limited Career Opportunities: Students with disabilities may encounter barriers to accessing career opportunities and pathways in technology fields. Discrimination, lack of accessibility accommodations, and misconceptions about their capabilities can limit their access to internships, job placements, and networking opportunities. Additionally, the underrepresentation of individuals with disabilities in STEM-related professions perpetuates systemic inequalities and limits the diversity of perspectives in the technology workforce.

Intersectional Challenges: Intersectionality, the intersection of multiple social identities and forms of oppression, exacerbates the challenges faced by students with disabilities. Students who belong to marginalized groups based on race, ethnicity, gender, sexual orientation, or socioeconomic status may experience compounded barriers and discrimination in technology education. Intersectional perspectives are essential for understanding the complex and interconnected nature of oppression and addressing the unique needs of diverse student populations.

Chapter 4

IMPORTANCE OF PROMOTING ACCESSIBILITY

In the realm of technology education, promoting accessibility isn't merely a moral imperative; it's the cornerstone of a truly equitable learning environment. Here are several compelling reasons why prioritizing accessibility is paramount:

Ensuring Equal Opportunities: Accessibility initiatives ensure that all students, regardless of their abilities, have equal opportunities to access and benefit from technology education. By removing barriers to learning, accessibility fosters an inclusive educational environment where every student can thrive.

Fostering Diversity and Inclusion: Promoting accessibility embraces the diversity of students' abilities and backgrounds, fostering a culture of inclusion where everyone feels valued and respected. This inclusive environment not only benefits students with disabilities but also enriches the educational experience for all students by exposing them to diverse perspectives and experiences.

Empowering Students with Disabilities: Accessible technology education empowers students with disabilities to fully participate in educational activities, develop their skills, and pursue their interests and career aspirations in technology-related fields. By providing the necessary support and accommodations, educators enable these students to unleash their full potential and contribute meaningfully to society.

Preparing for Real-world Challenges: In today's digital world, proficiency in technology is essential for success in education, employment, and everyday life. By promoting accessibility in technology education, educators equip students with the skills and knowledge they need to navigate an increasingly digital society and succeed in diverse academic and professional settings.

Meeting Legal and Ethical Obligations: Educational institutions have legal and ethical obligations to ensure that all students have equal access to educational opportunities. By promoting accessibility, schools and educators not only comply with disability rights laws such as the Americans with Disabilities Act (ADA) but also uphold principles of social justice and equity.

Enhancing Learning Outcomes: Accessible technology education benefits all students by removing barriers to learning and facilitating engagement, participation, and achievement. By adopting universal design principles and providing accommodations and modifications, educators can create learning environments that cater to diverse learning styles and needs, leading to improved learning outcomes for all students.

Promoting Innovation and Creativity: Accessibility challenges inspire innovation and creativity, driving the development of new technologies, tools, and teaching approaches that benefit students with disabilities and the broader educational community. By embracing accessibility as a priority, educators encourage a culture of innovation and problem-solving that benefits everyone.

Building a More Inclusive Society: Ultimately, promoting accessibility in technology education contributes to building a more inclusive society where everyone has the opportunity to contribute their talents and skills. By fostering empathy, understanding, and respect for individuals with disabilities, educators help cultivate a future where barriers to participation are eliminated, and diversity is celebrated.

Chapter 5

STRATEGIES FOR PROMOTING ACCESSIBILITY IN TECHNOLOGY EDUCATION

Accessibility in technology education is crucial for ensuring that all students, regardless of their abilities, have equal opportunities to learn and succeed. Implementing effective strategies can help educators create inclusive learning environments that meet the diverse needs of students with disabilities. Here are comprehensive strategies to promote accessibility:

1. **Raise Awareness and Understanding:** Educate stakeholders, including teachers, administrators, students, and parents, about the importance of accessibility in technology education. Offer training sessions, workshops, and informational materials to increase awareness and understanding of accessibility principles and best practices.

2. **Incorporate Universal Design for Learning (UDL):** Apply the principles of UDL to curriculum design, instruction, and assessment. Provide multiple means of representation, engagement, and expression to accommodate diverse learner needs and preferences.

3. **Provide Professional Development:** Offer ongoing professional development opportunities for teachers to enhance their knowledge and skills in

supporting students with disabilities. Training sessions should cover topics such as assistive technology, inclusive teaching practices, and accommodations.

4. Collaborate with Special Education Professionals: Foster collaboration between technology educators and special education professionals to develop inclusive teaching strategies and support systems for students with disabilities. Establish regular communication channels for sharing information and resources.

5. Implement Assistive Technologies: Integrate assistive technologies into the classroom to support students with disabilities in accessing and engaging with technology. Provide training and support for both teachers and students in using assistive technologies effectively.

6. Ensure Physical Accessibility: Ensure that technology classrooms and facilities are physically accessible to students with disabilities. Remove physical barriers, provide accessible seating arrangements, and ensure the availability of assistive devices and equipment.

7. Design Accessible Digital Content: Create digital content that is accessible to all students, including those with disabilities. Use accessible formats, such as alternative text for images, captions for videos, and structured headings for documents, to ensure that content is perceivable and navigable.

8. Offer Flexible Instructional Delivery: Provide flexible instructional delivery methods to accommodate diverse learning styles and preferences. Offer a combination of in-person, online, and hybrid instruction options to meet the needs of all students.

9. Provide Accommodations and Modifications: Offer accommodations and modifications to support students with disabilities in accessing and participating in technology education. Individualize instruction, assignments, and assessments based on students' unique needs and abilities.

10. Promote Inclusive Classroom Culture: Foster an inclusive classroom culture where all students feel valued, respected, and supported. Encourage collaboration, cooperation, and peer support among students with and without disabilities

11. Address Attitudes and Stereotypes: Challenge negative attitudes and stereotypes towards students with disabilities through education, awareness-raising, and positive role modelling. Promote a culture of acceptance, empathy, and inclusion among students and staff.

12. Provide Social and Emotional Support: Offer social and emotional support services to students with disabilities to address their unique needs and challenges. Provide counselling, mentoring, and peer support programs to promote mental health and well-being.

13. Engage Parents and Families: Involve parents and families in the technology education process by providing regular communication, support, and resources. Encourage parents to advocate for their child's needs and participate in decision-making processes.

14. Advocate for Policy Changes: Advocate for policy changes at the local, state, and national levels to support accessibility in technology education. Work with policymakers, advocacy groups, and other stakeholders to promote inclusive policies and allocate resources for accessibility initiatives.

15. Evaluate and Assess Accessibility: Regularly evaluate and assess the accessibility of technology education programs, practices, and resources. Use feedback from students, teachers, and stakeholders to identify areas for improvement and make necessary adjustments.

16. Provide Continuous Improvement: Continuously review and improve accessibility initiatives based on feedback, research, and best practices. Foster a culture of continuous improvement where educators are committed to making ongoing enhancements to support students with disabilities.

Chapter 6

ASSISTIVE TECHNOLOGIES IN TECHNOLOGY EDUCATION

Assistive technologies (AT) are transformative tools that empower students with disabilities to access and engage with technology education. This chapter explores the diverse range of assistive technologies available, their applications in the classroom, and strategies for effective integration.

Understanding Assistive Technologies: Assistive technologies encompass a broad spectrum of devices, software, and tools designed to support individuals with disabilities in various aspects of their lives. In the context of technology education, these technologies aim to remove barriers to learning and enhance students' abilities to participate fully in educational activities.

Types of Assistive Technologies

1. Alternative Input Devices: These include devices such as adapted keyboards, mouse alternatives (e.g., trackballs, touchpads), and switches that allow students with motor impairments to interact with computers and other digital devices effectively.

2. Screen Readers and Text-to-Speech Software: Screen reading software converts digital text into speech, enabling students with visual impairments to access

written content. Text-to-speech software also provides auditory feedback, supporting reading comprehension and writing tasks.

3. Screen Magnification Software: Screen magnifiers enlarge on-screen content, making it easier for students with low vision to read text, view images, and navigate digital interfaces.

4. Speech Recognition Software: Speech recognition technology allows students with physical disabilities or writing difficulties to dictate text and control computer functions using voice commands.

5. Braille Displays and Braille Translation Software: Braille displays convert digital text into Braille output, facilitating access to educational materials for students who are blind or have low vision.

6. Augmentative and Alternative Communication (AAC) Devices: AAC devices support students with communication disabilities by providing alternative means of expression, such as symbols, pictures, or text-to-speech output.

Applications in Technology Education

✓ Assistive technologies play a crucial role in enabling students with disabilities to participate fully in technology education. They support various aspects of learning, including:

- ✓ Access to Digital Content: Assistive technologies make it possible for students with disabilities to access digital textbooks, online resources, and educational software.

- ✓ Participation in Hands-On Activities: AT devices and software enable students to engage in hands-on activities such as coding, robotics, and multimedia production, fostering creativity and problem-solving skills.

- ✓ Communication and collaboration: AAC devices facilitate communication and collaboration among students with communication impairments, promoting social interaction and peer learning.

- ✓ Assessment and Evaluation: Assistive technologies support students during assessments by providing accommodations such as extended time, text-to-speech tools, or alternative response formats.

Integration Strategies

Successful integration of assistive technologies requires careful planning and collaboration among educators, students, and support professionals. Key strategies include:

Individualized Assessment: Conducting thorough assessments to identify students' specific needs and preferences regarding assistive technology.

Customization and Personalization: Tailoring assistive technology solutions to meet each student's unique requirements and learning goals.

Training and Support: Providing comprehensive training and ongoing technical support to students, teachers, and support staff to ensure effective use of assistive technologies.

Universal Design: Adopting universal design principles to create accessible learning environments that benefit all students, regardless of ability.

Collaboration with Specialists: Collaborating with assistive technology specialists, special educators, and other professionals to select, implement, and evaluate assistive technology solutions.

Ethical and Legal Considerations

It is essential to consider ethical and legal implications when implementing assistive technologies in technology education. This includes ensuring student privacy and confidentiality, adhering to relevant accessibility standards and guidelines (e.g., Section 508 of the Rehabilitation Act, Web Content Accessibility Guidelines), and promoting inclusive practices that respect students' autonomy and dignity.

Future Directions and Emerging Trends

Advancements in technology continue to expand the possibilities for assistive technologies in education. Emerging trends include the integration of artificial intelligence, virtual and augmented reality, and wearable devices to enhance accessibility and support personalized learning experiences for students with disabilities.

Chapter 7

INCLUSIVE CURRICULUM DESIGN

Inclusive curriculum design lies at the heart of promoting accessibility in technology education for students with disabilities. It involves intentionally creating learning experiences that accommodate diverse learning styles, abilities, and needs while maintaining high academic standards. This chapter delves into the principles, strategies, and practical considerations involved in designing a curriculum that fosters inclusivity and ensures equitable access for all learners.

Understanding Inclusive Curriculum Design

At its core, inclusive curriculum design aims to remove barriers to learning and participation while embracing diversity and promoting equity. It acknowledges that every student learns differently and that one-size-fits-all approaches are ineffective. Instead, it seeks to create flexible learning environments that can be tailored to meet the needs of individual students.

Key Principles of Inclusive Curriculum Design

1. **Universal Design for Learning (UDL):** UDL principles emphasize providing multiple means of representation, expression, and engagement to accommodate diverse learners. By offering various ways for students to access

content, demonstrate understanding, and engage with learning materials, educators can better address the needs of students with disabilities.

2. Differentiation: Differentiation involves modifying instruction, assignments, and assessments to meet the unique needs of each student. This may include providing alternative formats for materials, adjusting pacing or complexity, or offering additional support and scaffolding as needed.

3. Accessibility: Ensuring that all instructional materials, resources, and technologies are accessible to students with disabilities is essential. This involves considering factors such as readability, navigability, compatibility with assistive technologies, and adherence to accessibility standards.

4. Collaboration: Collaborating with special education professionals, support staff, and families is crucial for identifying student needs, developing individualized plans, and implementing effective strategies. By working together as a team, educators can better support students with disabilities in the classroom.

Strategies for inclusive curriculum design

1. **Flexible Instructional Delivery:** Offer a variety of instructional methods, including lectures, hands-on activities, multimedia presentations, and group discussions, to accommodate different learning preferences and abilities.

2. **Multiple Modalities:** Present information using multiple modalities, such as visual, auditory, and kinaesthetic, to ensure that all students can access content in ways that suit their learning styles and preferences.

3. **Scaffolded Learning:** Break down complex tasks into smaller, more manageable steps and provide scaffolding and support as students work towards mastery. This helps students build confidence and competence while minimizing frustration.

4. **Diverse Content Representation:** Incorporate diverse perspectives, experiences, and examples into the curriculum to make learning more relevant and inclusive for all students. Use a variety of resources, including texts, videos, and multimedia materials, to appeal to different interests and backgrounds.

5. **Assessment Flexibility**: Offer multiple options for demonstrating understanding and mastery, such as written assignments, oral presentations, projects, and hands-on demonstrations. Provide alternative assessment formats for students who may struggle with traditional methods.

6. **Technology Integration:** Leverage technology to enhance accessibility and support diverse learners. Utilize assistive technologies, such as screen readers,

text-to-speech software, and speech recognition tools, to remove barriers to learning and facilitate greater independence.

Practical Considerations for Implementation

1. Individualized Education Plans (IEPs) and 504 Plans: Collaborate with special education professionals to ensure that curriculum modifications and accommodations specified in students' IEPs or 504 plans are implemented effectively in the classroom.

2. Professional Development: Provide ongoing professional development opportunities for educators to learn about inclusive curriculum design principles, strategies, and best practices. Offer support and resources to help teachers effectively implement inclusive practices in their classrooms.

3. Accessible Materials and Resources: Ensure that all instructional materials, including textbooks, handouts, and digital resources, are accessible to students with disabilities. Provide training and support for educators on creating and selecting accessible materials.

4. Feedback and Reflection: Encourage regular feedback from students, families, and colleagues to evaluate the effectiveness of inclusive curriculum design strategies. Reflect on successes and challenges, and make adjustments as needed to better meet the needs of all learners.

Chapter 8

COLLABORATION WITH SPECIAL EDUCATION PROFESSIONALS

Collaboration between technology educators and special education professionals is pivotal in fostering inclusive learning environments for students with disabilities. This chapter delves into the significance of this partnership and outlines effective strategies for seamless collaboration.

Understanding the Partnership:

Begin by elucidating the roles of technology educators and special education professionals. Highlight how their distinct expertise can complement each other to address the diverse needs of students with disabilities.

Establishing Communication Channels:

Effective collaboration hinges on open communication channels. Discuss methods for establishing regular communication between technology educators and special education professionals, such as scheduled meetings, shared documents, and digital platforms.

Identifying Student Needs:

Special education professionals bring insights into the specific needs and accommodations required by students with disabilities. Explore methods for conducting assessments and collaborating to identify individual student needs within technology education settings.

Co-Planning and Co-Teaching:

Co-planning and co-teaching allow for the seamless integration of accommodations and modifications within technology lessons. Discuss strategies for jointly planning lessons, adapting instructional materials, and co-teaching in inclusive classrooms.

Professional Development Opportunities:

Both technology educators and special education professionals can benefit from targeted professional development opportunities. Explore ways to facilitate joint training sessions, workshops, and conferences to enhance collaborative practices and build a shared understanding of accessibility in technology education.

Data Sharing and Progress Monitoring:

Collaboration involves continuous monitoring of student progress and sharing relevant data between stakeholders. Discuss protocols for collecting and sharing student data, tracking progress towards individualized goals, and making data-informed decisions to support student learning.

Addressing Challenges and Conflict Resolution:

Despite best intentions, challenges may arise in collaborative efforts. Address common challenges, such as conflicting priorities or communication barriers, and provide strategies for constructive conflict resolution to ensure the partnership remains effective and sustainable.

Celebrating Successes and Sharing Best Practices:

Highlight the importance of celebrating successes and sharing best practices within the collaboration. Showcase examples of successful collaborative efforts between technology educators and special education professionals, and encourage educators to reflect on their experiences and lessons learned.

Chapter 9

TRAINING AND PROFESSIONAL DEVELOPMENT FOR TEACHERS

In the pursuit of creating inclusive and accessible technology education environments, the role of training and professional development for teachers cannot be overstated. This chapter delves into the essential components of training and ongoing professional development necessary for educators to effectively support students with disabilities in technology education.

Understanding the Need for Training:

Training is the cornerstone of empowering educators to meet the diverse needs of students with disabilities. This section highlights the critical importance of understanding the unique challenges faced by students with disabilities in technology education and the necessity of tailored training to address these challenges.

Key Components of Effective Training:

1. Foundational Knowledge: Educators must develop a foundational understanding of various disabilities, assistive technologies, and best practices in inclusive education. Training sessions should cover topics such as the types of disabilities, common barriers to access, and available assistive technologies.

2. Pedagogical Strategies: Training should equip teachers with practical strategies for adapting instructional methods, assessments, and classroom materials to meet the diverse learning needs of students with disabilities. This includes differentiated instruction, Universal Design for Learning (UDL) principles, and the use of assistive technologies.

3. Collaboration Skills: Effective collaboration between general education and special education teachers is paramount in promoting accessibility. Training should emphasize collaboration strategies, communication techniques, and the importance of interdisciplinary teamwork.

4. Accessibility Tools and Resources: Educators need exposure to a variety of accessibility tools and resources to effectively support students with disabilities. Training sessions should introduce educators to assistive technologies, accessible digital content creation tools, and resources for designing inclusive curriculum.

5. Legal and Ethical Considerations: Teachers must be aware of their legal obligations and ethical responsibilities in providing equitable access to education for students with disabilities. Training should cover relevant legislation such as the Individuals with Disabilities Education Act (IDEA) and Section 504 of the Rehabilitation Act.

Modes of Delivery:

Training and professional development can be delivered through a variety of modes to accommodate different learning styles and preferences:

- ✓ Workshops and Seminars: Interactive workshops and seminars provide opportunities for hands-on learning, group discussions, and collaboration among educators.

- ✓ Online Courses and Webinars: Virtual courses and webinars offer flexibility and accessibility, allowing educators to engage in professional development at their own pace and convenience.

- ✓ Peer Learning Communities: Establishing peer learning communities or professional learning networks enables educators to share knowledge, experiences, and best practices related to accessibility in technology education.

- ✓ Coaching and Mentoring: Individualized coaching and mentoring provide personalized support and guidance to educators as they implement accessibility strategies in their classrooms.

Sustaining Professional Development:

Sustainability of professional development efforts is essential for long-term impact. Strategies for sustaining professional development include:

- ✓ Continuous Learning Opportunities: Encourage educators to pursue ongoing learning opportunities through conferences, workshops, and online courses focused on accessibility and inclusive education.

- ✓ Embedded Professional Development: Integrate accessibility training into existing professional development programs and initiatives to ensure continuity and relevance.

- ✓ Collaborative Learning Communities: Foster communities of practice where educators can continue to collaborate, share resources, and support each other in implementing accessibility strategies.

- ✓ Feedback and Reflection: Provide mechanisms for educators to reflect on their practice, receive feedback from peers and mentors, and adjust their approach based on insights gained from experience.

Chapter 10

CREATING ACCESSIBLE DIGITAL CONTENT

In an increasingly digital world, creating accessible digital content is paramount to ensuring that all students, including those with disabilities, can fully participate in technology education. This chapter delves into the principles and practices of designing digital content that is inclusive and accessible.

Understanding Accessibility in Digital Content: Accessibility in digital content refers to designing materials in a way that allows individuals with disabilities to perceive, understand, navigate, and interact with the content effectively. This section explores the various types of disabilities that can affect digital accessibility, including visual, auditory, motor, and cognitive impairments.

Guidelines and Standards for Accessibility: Several guidelines and standards have been developed to help creators ensure that their digital content is accessible. This section introduces key accessibility standards such as the Web Content Accessibility Guidelines (WCAG) and discusses how they can be applied to create accessible technology education materials.

Principles of Accessible Design: Accessible design principles form the foundation for creating digital content that is usable by all learners. This section explores principles such as perceivability, operability, understandability, and robustness, and provides examples of how they can be implemented in technology education materials.

Making Multimedia Content Accessible: Multimedia content, including videos, audio recordings, and interactive media, presents unique challenges for accessibility. This section discusses strategies for making multimedia content accessible, such as providing captions and transcripts for videos and ensuring compatibility with screen readers.

Designing Accessible Documents and Presentations: Documents and presentations are commonly used in technology education to convey information and instructions. This section explores best practices for creating accessible documents and presentations, including using proper heading structure, alternative text for images, and accessible slide design.

Ensuring Navigation and Interaction Accessibility: Navigation and interaction are critical aspects of digital content usability. This section discusses techniques for ensuring that navigation menus, links, forms, and interactive elements are accessible to individuals using assistive technologies.

Testing and Evaluating Accessibility: Testing and evaluating digital content for accessibility is essential to ensure that it meets the needs of all users. This section explores methods for testing accessibility, including manual testing, automated tools, and user testing with individuals with disabilities.

Addressing Common Accessibility Challenges: Despite best efforts, creators may encounter challenges in achieving full accessibility in digital content. This section addresses common accessibility challenges such as complex layouts, inaccessible third-party content, and compatibility issues with assistive technologies, and provides solutions for overcoming these challenges.

Promoting a Culture of Accessibility: Creating accessible digital content is not just a technical endeavour but also a cultural one. This section discusses the importance of fostering a culture of accessibility within educational institutions and provides strategies for promoting awareness and training among content creators.

Resources and Tools for Creating Accessible Content: Numerous resources and tools are available to support creators in designing accessible digital content. This section highlights resources such as accessibility guidelines, training materials, and software tools that can facilitate the creation of inclusive technology education materials.

Creating accessible digital content is not only a legal requirement but also a moral imperative to ensure equitable access to education for all students. By following the principles and practices outlined in this chapter, educators can play a crucial role in promoting accessibility and fostering an inclusive learning environment in technology education.

Chapter 11

UNIVERSAL DESIGN PRINCIPLES IN TECHNOLOGY EDUCATION

Universal Design Principles are fundamental in ensuring that technology education is accessible to all students, regardless of their abilities. By adopting these principles, educators can create inclusive learning environments that accommodate diverse learning styles and needs. This chapter explores the key principles of Universal Design and their application in technology education:

1. **Equitable Use**: Technology education should be designed to be usable by all students, ensuring that no one is disadvantaged due to their abilities. This principle emphasizes the importance of providing equal access to learning opportunities for students with disabilities.

2. **Flexibility in Use:** Technology tools and resources should offer multiple ways for students to engage with content and demonstrate their understanding. Flexibility in use allows students to choose the tools and methods that best suit their individual needs and preferences.

3. **Simple and Intuitive Use:** Technology should be easy to understand and navigate for all students, including those with cognitive or learning disabilities.

Designing technology education materials and resources with simplicity and intuitiveness in mind enhances accessibility for everyone.

4. Perceptible Information: Information presented in technology education should be perceivable by all students, regardless of their sensory abilities. Providing alternative formats, such as audio descriptions or tactile graphics, ensures that information is accessible to students with visual or auditory impairments.

5. Tolerance for Error: Technology tools should be forgiving of mistakes, allowing students to learn and explore without fear of failure. Tolerance for error encourages experimentation and promotes a growth mindset among students with disabilities.

6. Low Physical Effort: Physical tasks and interactions in technology education should require minimal effort, making them accessible to students with mobility impairments or other physical disabilities. This principle emphasizes the importance of ergonomic design and accessible interfaces.

7. Size and Space for Approach and Use: Technology environments should be designed to accommodate students of all sizes and abilities. Providing ample space and adjustable equipment ensures that students can comfortably access and interact with technology tools.

8. **Aesthetic and Minimalist Design:** The design of technology education materials should be aesthetically pleasing while avoiding unnecessary complexity. Aesthetic and minimalist design promotes focus and reduces cognitive overload for students with disabilities.

9. **Community of Learners:** Foster a sense of community and collaboration among students in technology education. Encouraging peer support and cooperative learning creates an inclusive learning environment where students with disabilities feel valued and included.

10. **Instructional Climate:** Create an instructional climate that is supportive and respectful of diverse learning needs. Technology educators should be proactive in addressing barriers and accommodating individual differences to ensure that all students can participate fully in learning activities.

11. **Accessible Assessment:** Assessment methods and tools should be designed to be accessible to all students, allowing them to demonstrate their knowledge and skills effectively. Providing alternative assessment formats and accommodations ensures that students with disabilities are not unfairly disadvantaged in the evaluation process.

Chapter 12

PROVIDING ACCOMMODATIONS AND MODIFICATIONS

In the pursuit of inclusive technology education, it's imperative to acknowledge the diverse needs of students with disabilities and provide appropriate accommodations and modifications to ensure their success. Accommodations and modifications serve as tools to level the playing field, allowing students with disabilities to fully participate in technology education alongside their peers. This chapter delves into the distinction between accommodations and modifications, explores various strategies for implementation, and emphasizes the importance of individualized support.

Understanding Accommodations and Modifications: Accommodations and modifications are often used interchangeably, but they serve distinct purposes. Accommodations refer to changes in how students access information or demonstrate their learning without altering the curriculum's content. Examples include extended time on assessments, preferential seating, or the provision of assistive technology devices. On the other hand, modifications involve altering the curriculum's content, making it more accessible or aligning it with a student's abilities. This could entail simplifying assignments, adjusting grading criteria, or providing alternative learning materials.

Creating Individualized Accommodation Plans: Effective accommodation and modification plans are tailored to meet the unique needs of each student. Collaborating with special education professionals, parents, and the students themselves is essential in identifying necessary accommodations and modifications. Conducting thorough assessments to understand students' strengths, challenges, and preferences can inform the development of personalized plans that maximize their learning potential. Regular reviews and adjustments ensure that accommodations remain relevant and effective as students' needs evolve.

Implementing Accommodations and Modifications: Implementing accommodations and modifications requires careful planning and coordination among educators and support staff. Teachers must be knowledgeable about the accommodations outlined in students' Individualized Education Programs (IEPs) or 504 plans and be prepared to implement them consistently. Providing training and resources to educators on how to effectively implement accommodations and modifications fosters a supportive learning environment where all students can thrive. Flexibility and creativity in adapting instructional methods and materials further enhance the effectiveness of accommodations and modifications.

Promoting Independence and Self-Advocacy: While accommodations and modifications offer essential support, it's crucial to empower students to advocate for their needs and develop self-management skills. Encouraging students to communicate their preferences, challenges, and successes fosters a sense of ownership over their learning journey. Teaching self-advocacy skills equips students with the confidence and strategies to effectively navigate academic settings and advocate for reasonable accommodations as they transition to higher education or the workforce.

Ensuring Equity and Inclusion: Providing accommodations and modifications is not merely about compliance; it's about fostering an inclusive learning environment where all students feel valued and supported. Educators must guard against stigmatizing students who require accommodations and promote a culture of acceptance and understanding. By emphasizing the principle of equity, educators can create a classroom culture where individual differences are celebrated, and every student has the opportunity to reach their full potential.

Measuring Effectiveness and Adjusting Strategies: Regular assessment of the effectiveness of accommodations and modifications is essential to ensure that they meet students' needs and promote academic success. Collecting feedback from students, parents, and educators allows for ongoing refinement of accommodation plans. Analysing academic performance data can also provide insights into the impact of accommodations on student outcomes. Flexibility in adjusting strategies based on student progress and feedback is key to continuously improving the effectiveness of accommodations and modifications.

Chapter 13

ENSURING PHYSICAL ACCESSIBILITY IN TECHNOLOGY CLASSROOMS

Physical accessibility is a cornerstone of creating inclusive technology classrooms where students with disabilities can fully participate and engage in learning. This chapter explores the various aspects of physical accessibility and provides practical strategies for ensuring that technology classrooms are welcoming and accommodating to all students.

Understanding Physical Barriers: Firstly, it's crucial to identify and understand the physical barriers that may exist in technology classrooms. These barriers can include inaccessible classroom layouts, narrow doorways, high countertops, and inadequate seating arrangements. By conducting a thorough assessment of the physical environment, educators can pinpoint areas that require modifications to enhance accessibility.

Adapting Classroom Layouts: One of the primary steps in ensuring physical accessibility is to adapt the classroom layout to accommodate students with diverse needs. This may involve rearranging furniture to create wider pathways for wheelchair users, ensuring that all equipment and materials are within reach, and providing flexible seating options to accommodate different mobility requirements.

Accessible Workstations and Equipment: Technology classrooms often feature a variety of equipment and tools essential for hands-on learning experiences. It's essential to ensure that these workstations and equipment are designed with accessibility in mind. For example, adjustable-height tables can accommodate students who use wheelchairs, while ergonomic tools and devices can support students with mobility impairments.

Accessible Materials and Resources: In addition to physical space considerations, technology educators should also focus on making instructional materials and resources accessible to all students. This includes providing alternative formats such as large print, braille, or digital text for students with visual impairments, as well as ensuring that audiovisual materials are captioned or accompanied by transcripts for students with hearing impairments.

Promoting Safety and Independence: Safety is paramount in technology classrooms, and it's essential to ensure that all students can navigate the space safely and independently. This may involve installing grab bars or handrails in key areas, providing clear signage and wayfinding cues, and offering assistance devices such as reachers or adapted tools to support students in completing tasks safely.

Staff Training and Awareness: Educators and staff play a crucial role in maintaining a physically accessible environment in technology classrooms. Providing training on disability awareness, inclusive practices, and assistive technologies can empower educators to proactively address accessibility issues and support students with disabilities effectively.

Collaboration with Accessibility Experts: Collaborating with accessibility experts, such as occupational therapists or disability service providers, can provide valuable insights and guidance on creating physically accessible technology classrooms. These professionals can offer recommendations for accommodations, modifications, and assistive technologies tailored to the specific needs of students with disabilities.

Regular Maintenance and Evaluation: Ensuring physical accessibility is an ongoing process that requires regular maintenance and evaluation. Technology educators should routinely assess the classroom environment, solicit feedback from students with disabilities, and make necessary adjustments to address emerging accessibility issues.

Fostering a Culture of Inclusivity: Ultimately, promoting physical accessibility in technology classrooms is not just about making structural changes—it's about fostering a culture of inclusivity where all students feel valued and respected. By modelling inclusive behaviour, celebrating diversity, and promoting empathy and understanding, educators can create an environment where every student can thrive.

Chapter 14

ADDRESSING ATTITUDES AND STEREOTYPES

Attitudes and stereotypes can profoundly influence the educational experiences of students with disabilities in technology classrooms. Negative attitudes and misconceptions not only create barriers to learning but also contribute to the marginalization and exclusion of these students. Addressing attitudes and stereotypes is essential for fostering an inclusive learning environment where all students feel valued and respected. In this chapter, we delve into the impact of attitudes and stereotypes on accessibility in technology education and explore strategies for promoting positive attitudes and challenging harmful stereotypes.

Understanding Attitudes and Stereotypes: Attitudes refer to individuals' feelings, beliefs, and predispositions towards certain groups or individuals. Stereotypes are oversimplified and often inaccurate beliefs about a particular group of people. In the context of technology education, attitudes and stereotypes may manifest as assumptions about the capabilities, intelligence, or potential of students with disabilities. These attitudes can lead to lowered expectations, discrimination, and limited opportunities for students with disabilities.

The Impact of Attitudes and Stereotypes: Negative attitudes and stereotypes can have profound effects on students with disabilities. They may experience feelings of inferiority, self-doubt, and alienation, which can hinder their academic and social development. Additionally, negative attitudes among peers and educators can create a hostile learning environment, further exacerbating the challenges faced by students with disabilities.

Strategies for Promoting Positive Attitudes

1. **Education and Awareness:** Educating students, educators, and the broader school community about disability rights, diversity, and inclusion can help challenge stereotypes and foster empathy and understanding.

2. **Promoting Disability Representation:** Incorporating diverse perspectives and representations of individuals with disabilities in curriculum materials, classroom discussions, and media can challenge stereotypes and promote positive attitudes.

3. **Encouraging Personal Connections:** Encouraging students to interact with peers with disabilities in meaningful ways can help break down barriers and foster positive relationships based on mutual respect and understanding.

4. **Modelling Inclusive Behaviour:** Educators can model inclusive behaviour by treating all students with respect, valuing diversity, and creating opportunities for collaboration and participation.

5. **Promoting Strengths-Based Approaches:** Emphasizing the strengths, abilities, and potential of students with disabilities can help shift attitudes from deficit-based to strengths-based perspectives.

Challenging Harmful Stereotypes:

1. **Providing Counterexamples:** Highlighting examples of individuals with disabilities who have achieved success in technology fields can challenge stereotypes and inspire students to pursue their passions.

2. **Fostering Critical Thinking**: Encouraging students to critically examine stereotypes and question assumptions can help them develop a more nuanced understanding of disability and diversity.

3. **Creating Inclusive Learning Environments:** Designing technology classrooms that are welcoming, inclusive, and supportive of diversity can challenge stereotypes and promote positive attitudes among students and educators alike.

4. **Addressing Implicit Bias:** Educators should reflect on their own biases and work to address implicit bias in their interactions with students with disabilities, ensuring fair and equitable treatment for all learners.

Chapter 15

PROMOTING INCLUSIVE CLASSROOM CULTURE

Creating an inclusive classroom culture is fundamental to fostering an environment where all students, including those with disabilities, feel valued, respected, and empowered to participate fully in technology education. A classroom culture that embraces diversity and promotes inclusivity not only benefits students with disabilities but enriches the educational experience for all learners. In this chapter, we explore strategies and practices for promoting an inclusive classroom culture in technology education.

Understanding Inclusive Classroom Culture: To cultivate an inclusive classroom culture, it's essential to first understand what it entails. Inclusive classroom culture goes beyond mere tolerance; it celebrates diversity, encourages collaboration, and embraces the unique strengths and abilities of each student. It involves creating a sense of belonging where every student feels accepted, supported, and appreciated for who they are.

Establishing Classroom Norms and Expectations: Setting clear norms and expectations is key to creating a positive and inclusive learning environment. Collaboratively establish classroom norms with input from all students, emphasizing the importance of mutual respect, active listening, and open-mindedness. Ensure that these norms are consistently reinforced and upheld throughout the school year.

Promoting Positive Interactions and Peer Relationships: Encourage positive interactions and foster meaningful peer relationships within the classroom. Provide opportunities for collaborative learning, group projects, and peer mentoring initiatives that promote teamwork and mutual support among students. Model inclusive behaviour and provide guidance on effective communication and conflict resolution strategies.

Celebrating Diversity and Recognizing Strengths: Celebrate the diversity of your classroom by incorporating diverse perspectives, experiences, and cultural backgrounds into your teaching materials and activities. Highlight the unique strengths and talents of each student, including those with disabilities, and create opportunities for students to share their interests and experiences with their peers.

Addressing Bias and Challenging Stereotypes: Address implicit biases and challenge stereotypes that may exist within the classroom. Foster discussions around diversity, equity, and inclusion, encouraging students to critically examine their assumptions and perspectives. Provide resources and literature that showcase diverse role models and challenge traditional stereotypes in technology fields.

Creating a Safe and Supportive Learning Environment: Ensure that your classroom environment is physically and emotionally safe for all students. Consider the physical layout of the classroom to accommodate diverse needs, such as wheelchair accessibility and sensory-friendly spaces. Implement strategies to support students' emotional well-being, such as mindfulness activities, check-in routines, and access to counselling resources.

Empowering Student Voice and Agency: Empower students to take ownership of their learning and contribute to decision-making processes within the classroom. Provide opportunities for student voice and agency through class discussions, student-led projects, and feedback mechanisms that allow students to express their thoughts, concerns, and ideas for improvement.

Providing Differentiated Instruction and Support: Differentiate instruction to meet the diverse needs of all learners, including students with disabilities. Utilize a variety of instructional strategies, materials, and technologies to accommodate different learning styles and abilities. Provide individualized support and accommodations as needed, ensuring that all students have equitable access to learning opportunities.

Fostering Empathy and Understanding: Promote empathy and understanding among students by encouraging them to walk in each other's shoes and consider perspectives different from their own. Incorporate literature, media, and real-life examples that highlight the experiences of individuals with disabilities and promote empathy-building activities that foster compassion and understanding.

Collaborating with Support Services and Specialists: Collaborate with special education professionals, support services, and specialists to provide comprehensive support for students with disabilities. Seek input from experts in assistive technology, speech therapy, occupational therapy, and other relevant fields to ensure that students receive the individualized support they need to succeed.

Promoting Peer Support and Mentorship: Facilitate peer support networks and mentorship programs that pair students with disabilities with supportive peers or older mentors who can provide guidance, encouragement, and friendship. Foster a culture of inclusion and peer support where students look out for one another and offer assistance when needed.

Encouraging Reflective Practice and Growth Mindset: Encourage reflective practice and a growth mindset among students, emphasizing the value of perseverance, resilience, and continuous learning. Provide opportunities for students to reflect on their own biases, assumptions, and areas for growth, and celebrate their progress and achievements along their learning journey.

Engaging Families and Caregivers: Engage families and caregivers as partners in promoting an inclusive classroom culture. Communicate regularly with parents/guardians about classroom activities, student progress, and opportunities for involvement. Seek input from families on ways to support their child's unique needs and celebrate their contributions to the classroom community.

Promoting Accessibility and Universal Design: Promote accessibility and universal design principles throughout the classroom environment, curriculum, and instructional materials. Ensure that technology tools, learning resources, and physical spaces are accessible to all students, including those with disabilities, and actively involve students in the co-design of accessible learning experiences.

Measuring and Monitoring Inclusivity: Regularly assess and monitor the inclusivity of your classroom culture through feedback mechanisms, student surveys, and observational data. Use assessment data to identify areas for improvement and refine your practices to better meet the needs of all learners. Celebrate successes and acknowledge progress toward creating a more inclusive learning environment.

Chapter 16

SUPPORTING SOCIAL AND EMOTIONAL WELL-BEING

In the pursuit of accessibility in technology education, it's imperative to recognize and address the social and emotional well-being of students with disabilities. This chapter delves into the multifaceted aspects of supporting their emotional and social needs within the educational framework.

Understanding Social and Emotional Needs: Students with disabilities often encounter social and emotional challenges that can impact their learning experiences. These challenges may arise from feelings of isolation, frustration with academic tasks, or negative perceptions from peers and educators. Understanding these needs is the first step toward providing effective support.

Creating a Supportive Environment: Building a supportive environment begins with fostering a culture of acceptance and empathy within the classroom. Educators can facilitate open discussions about disability, promote positive peer interactions, and discourage bullying or discrimination. By creating a safe space where students feel valued and respected, social and emotional well-being can flourish.

Building Self-esteem and Confidence: Students with disabilities may struggle with self-esteem and confidence due to perceived limitations or past experiences of failure. Educators can play a crucial role in nurturing their self-esteem by providing encouragement, celebrating their achievements, and offering constructive feedback. Emphasizing their strengths and abilities helps bolster confidence and fosters a growth mindset.

Teaching Coping Strategies: Coping strategies empower students to navigate challenges and regulate their emotions effectively. Educators can teach practical coping techniques such as deep breathing exercises, mindfulness practices, or cognitive-behavioural strategies. These tools equip students with the resilience to overcome obstacles and manage stressors in their academic journey.

Promoting Peer Support Networks: Peer support networks offer valuable social and emotional support for students with disabilities. Educators can facilitate peer mentorship programs, group activities, or buddy systems where students can connect with peers who share similar experiences. These peer relationships provide a sense of belonging and understanding, reducing feelings of isolation and fostering meaningful connections.

Encouraging Self-Advocacy: Empowering students to advocate for their own needs is essential for their social and emotional well-being. Educators can teach self-advocacy skills such as articulating their learning preferences, requesting accommodations, or seeking support when needed. By fostering self-advocacy, students develop a sense of agency and autonomy in their educational journey.

Collaborating with Support Services: Collaboration with support services such as school counsellors, psychologists, or special education professionals enhances the support available to students with disabilities. Educators can work collaboratively to identify students' social and emotional needs, develop personalized interventions, and provide ongoing support. Leveraging the expertise of support services ensures a holistic approach to addressing students' well-being.

Family Engagement and Support: Family engagement plays a crucial role in supporting the social and emotional well-being of students with disabilities. Educators can involve families in the educational process, communicate regularly about students' progress, and provide resources for support outside the classroom. By partnering with families, educators create a united front in nurturing students' overall well-being.

Monitoring Progress and Adjustment: Regular monitoring of students' social and emotional well-being allows educators to assess the effectiveness of support strategies and make necessary adjustments. Educators can use observation, check-ins, and feedback from students and families to evaluate progress and identify areas for improvement. Flexibility and responsiveness ensure that support measures remain tailored to students' evolving needs.

Promoting a Culture of Empathy and Inclusion: At the heart of supporting social and emotional well-being is a culture of empathy and inclusion. Educators can model empathetic behaviour, promote acceptance of individual differences, and challenge stereotypes and biases. By fostering a culture of empathy and inclusion, educators cultivate an environment where all students feel valued, respected, and supported.

Chapter 17

PARENT AND FAMILY ENGAGEMENT

Engaging parents and families are paramount in supporting students with disabilities in technology education. This chapter delves into the significance of fostering strong partnerships between educators, families, and caregivers to enhance the educational journey of students with disabilities.

Understanding the Role of Parents and Families: Parents and families are integral stakeholders in a student's educational journey. For students with disabilities, their support and involvement can significantly impact academic success, especially in technology education. Understanding the unique challenges and experiences of families with children who have disabilities is essential for building effective engagement strategies.

Creating Collaborative Partnerships: Effective parent and family engagement begins with establishing collaborative partnerships between educators and families. This section explores strategies for building trust, open communication, and mutual respect between educators and parents. By fostering positive relationships, educators can create a supportive network that enhances the overall learning experience for students with disabilities.

Providing Resources and Support: Many parents and families may feel overwhelmed or uncertain about how to support their child's technology education, particularly if their child has a disability. Providing access to resources, workshops, and support groups can empower parents and families to become active participants in their child's learning journey. This section discusses the importance of offering relevant resources and guidance to assist families in navigating the educational landscape effectively.

Individualized Support Plans: Collaborating with parents and families to develop individualized support plans is crucial for meeting the diverse needs of students with disabilities. This section explores the process of developing personalized education plans (IEPs) or 504 plans in collaboration with families, ensuring that technology education goals align with the student's unique strengths, challenges, and aspirations.

Promoting Home-School Connections: Technology education shouldn't be confined to the classroom—it should extend into the home environment as well. This section explores ways to promote home-school connections by providing families with opportunities to reinforce learning, access educational technology tools, and engage in meaningful activities that support their child's technological literacy.

Empowering Advocacy Skills: Empowering parents and families with advocacy skills is essential for ensuring that students with disabilities receive the support and accommodations they need to thrive in technology education. This section discusses strategies for equipping families with the knowledge, confidence, and resources to advocate effectively on behalf of their child's educational rights and needs.

Celebrating Achievements and Progress: Recognizing and celebrating the achievements and progress of students with disabilities is essential for fostering a positive and inclusive learning environment. This section explores ways to involve parents and families in celebrating their child's successes, whether through parent-teacher conferences, showcases of student work, or other collaborative events that highlight student accomplishments in technology education.

Addressing Concerns and Challenges: Open communication channels between educators and families are vital for addressing concerns and challenges that may arise throughout the educational journey. This section explores strategies for actively listening to and addressing the concerns of parents and families, fostering a collaborative approach to problem-solving and decision-making.

Cultural Competence and Diversity: Recognizing and respecting the diversity of families is essential for effective parent and family engagement. This section explores the importance of cultural competence in engaging families from diverse backgrounds, acknowledging the unique cultural, linguistic, and socio-economic factors that may influence family involvement in their child's technology education.

Building a Supportive Community: Creating a supportive community that values and prioritizes parent and family engagement is essential for promoting the success of students with disabilities in technology education. This section explores strategies for fostering a sense of belonging and inclusivity within the school community, encouraging active participation and collaboration among all stakeholders.

Chapter 18

ADVOCACY FOR ACCESSIBILITY IN TECHNOLOGY EDUCATION

Advocacy serves as the cornerstone for fostering systemic change and ensuring that accessibility becomes a priority in technology education. This chapter delves into the strategies and methodologies for advocating at various levels to promote inclusivity in educational settings.

Understanding the Advocacy Landscape: Begin by exploring the current landscape of accessibility advocacy in technology education. Highlight the existing challenges, gaps, and successes in advocating for inclusive practices.

Policy Advocacy: Examine the role of policy advocacy in driving accessibility initiatives. Discuss key legislation such as the Individuals with Disabilities Education Act (IDEA), Section 504 of the Rehabilitation Act, and the Americans with Disabilities Act (ADA). Analyse how these laws impact accessibility in technology education and explore avenues for strengthening policy frameworks.

Collaborative Advocacy: Advocacy thrives on collaboration. Explore the importance of forming alliances with stakeholders such as educators, administrators, parents, students, disability rights organizations, and policymakers. Highlight successful collaborative advocacy efforts and discuss strategies for building coalitions to amplify the voices advocating for accessibility.

Community Engagement: Community engagement is a powerful tool for raising awareness and garnering support for accessibility initiatives. Discuss the importance of engaging with local communities, hosting workshops, organizing awareness campaigns, and leveraging social media platforms to mobilize support for inclusive technology education.

Professional Development and Training: Advocacy efforts can be bolstered by equipping educators with the knowledge and skills to champion accessibility. Explore the role of professional development and training programs in empowering educators to advocate for inclusive practices. Provide resources and strategies for integrating accessibility advocacy into teacher training curricula.

Data-Driven Advocacy: Data serves as a compelling tool for advocacy, providing evidence of the impact of accessibility initiatives on student outcomes. Discuss the importance of collecting and analysing data related to accessibility in technology education, such as student performance metrics, graduation rates, and access to assistive technologies. Explore how data can be leveraged to advocate for increased resources and support for accessibility initiatives.

Legislative Advocacy: Legislative advocacy involves influencing policymakers to enact laws and policies that promote accessibility in technology education.

Discuss strategies for engaging with legislators, drafting policy proposals, and advocating for legislative changes to address gaps in accessibility.

Media Advocacy: The media plays a crucial role in shaping public opinion and driving social change. Explore the importance of media advocacy in raising awareness about accessibility issues in technology education. Discuss strategies for leveraging traditional media outlets, social media platforms, and digital storytelling to amplify the voices of students, educators, and advocates.

Intersectional Advocacy: Acknowledge the intersectionality of accessibility advocacy by considering the unique needs of diverse student populations. Explore how advocacy efforts can address the intersection of disability with other forms of marginalization, such as race, gender, socioeconomic status, and language proficiency.

Global Advocacy: Accessibility in technology education is a global issue that requires collective action on a global scale. Discuss the importance of international collaboration and advocacy networks in promoting inclusive practices worldwide. Highlight successful global advocacy initiatives and explore opportunities for cross-cultural exchange and learning.

Measuring Impact and Success: Evaluate the impact of advocacy efforts by assessing changes in policy, practice, and attitudes towards accessibility in technology education. Discuss metrics for measuring success, such as increased access to assistive technologies, improved graduation rates for students with disabilities, and enhanced support for inclusive curriculum design.

Sustaining Advocacy Efforts: Advocacy is an ongoing process that requires sustained commitment and perseverance. Discuss strategies for sustaining advocacy efforts over the long term, such as building grassroots movements, cultivating leadership pipelines, and fostering a culture of inclusivity within educational institutions.

Case Studies and Success Stories: Illustrate the power of advocacy through real-world case studies and success stories. Highlight examples of successful advocacy campaigns, policy reforms, and collaborative initiatives that have resulted in tangible improvements in accessibility in technology education.

Empowering Student Advocates: Empower students with disabilities to become advocates for accessibility in technology education. Discuss strategies for fostering self-advocacy skills, providing opportunities for student leadership, and amplifying the voices of students in advocacy efforts.

Ethical Considerations in Advocacy: Navigate the ethical considerations involved in advocacy for accessibility in technology education. Discuss principles of social justice, equity, and inclusivity, and explore how advocacy efforts can uphold these principles while respecting the rights and dignity of all stakeholders.

Chapter 19

EVALUATING AND ASSESSING ACCESSIBILITY

Assessing the accessibility of technology education programs is crucial for ensuring that they effectively meet the needs of students with disabilities. This chapter explores methods for evaluating and assessing accessibility initiatives, providing educators with tools to measure progress and identify areas for improvement.

Understanding Accessibility Evaluation: Before diving into evaluation methods, it's essential to understand what accessibility encompasses in the context of technology education. Accessibility evaluation involves assessing various aspects, including physical access to technology, the usability of digital content, availability of assistive technologies, and the inclusivity of instructional practices.

Frameworks and Guidelines: Several frameworks and guidelines exist to assist educators in evaluating accessibility. One prominent example is the Web Content Accessibility Guidelines (WCAG), which provide standards for web accessibility. Additionally, frameworks like the Universal Design for Learning (UDL) offer principles for designing inclusive learning environments. Understanding and applying these frameworks can guide educators in their assessment efforts.

Assessment Tools and Checklists: Numerous assessment tools and checklists are available to help educators evaluate accessibility in technology education. These tools may focus on different aspects, such as website accessibility, software usability, or physical classroom accessibility. Educators can utilize these resources to conduct thorough evaluations and identify areas needing improvement.

User Testing and Feedback: Direct feedback from students with disabilities is invaluable in assessing accessibility. Conducting user testing sessions where students interact with technology and provide feedback can uncover usability issues and accessibility barriers that may not be apparent through traditional evaluation methods. This participatory approach empowers students to contribute to the improvement of technology education programs.

Data Collection and Analysis: Collecting data on accessibility metrics is essential for tracking progress and making informed decisions. This may involve gathering quantitative data, such as the number of accessible digital resources available or the percentage of classrooms meeting physical accessibility standards. Qualitative data, such as feedback from students and educators, can provide valuable insights into the lived experiences of individuals with disabilities.

Continuous Improvement: Evaluation should be an ongoing process, integrated into the continuous improvement cycle of technology education programs. Regularly assessing accessibility, analysing data, and soliciting feedback allows educators to make iterative improvements over time. Embracing a mindset of continuous improvement ensures that accessibility remains a priority and that efforts are responsive to evolving needs and challenges.

Collaboration and Stakeholder Involvement: Involving stakeholders in the evaluation process fosters collaboration and ensures that diverse perspectives are considered. This may include students, parents, educators, special education professionals, and disability advocates. Collaborative evaluation efforts promote transparency, accountability, and shared ownership of accessibility initiatives.

Addressing Findings and Implementing Solutions: Once evaluation results are obtained, it's essential to take action to address identified issues and implement solutions. This may involve providing professional development for educators, updating curriculum materials, investing in assistive technologies, or making physical modifications to learning environments. By prioritizing and addressing evaluation findings, educators can create more accessible technology education programs.

Monitoring and Review: After implementing solutions, ongoing monitoring and review are necessary to ensure that improvements are effective and sustainable. This involves regularly revisiting evaluation metrics, soliciting feedback, and adjusting strategies as needed. By maintaining vigilance and responsiveness, educators can continuously enhance the accessibility of technology education for students with disabilities.

Chapter 20

FUNDING AND RESOURCES FOR ACCESSIBILITY INITIATIVES

Securing adequate funding and resources is paramount to the success of accessibility initiatives in technology education. Without proper financial support, schools and districts may struggle to implement necessary accommodations and provide essential tools for students with disabilities. This chapter explores various funding sources and strategies for maximizing resources to support accessibility initiatives effectively.

Understanding Funding Sources:

1. **Federal Grants:** Federal grants, such as those provided by the U.S. Department of Education, offer significant funding opportunities for accessibility initiatives in education. Programs like the Individuals with Disabilities Education Act (IDEA) provide funds specifically allocated for supporting students with disabilities.

2. **State Grants:** Many states offer grants and funding opportunities to support accessibility initiatives at the local level. These grants may be administered through state education agencies or other governmental organizations.

3. **Local Funding:** Local school districts may allocate funds from their budgets to support accessibility initiatives. Advocacy efforts at the local level can help ensure that accessibility remains a priority in budget planning.

4. **Corporate Sponsorship:** Partnering with corporations and technology companies can provide additional funding and resources for accessibility initiatives. Companies often have corporate social responsibility programs or grant opportunities focused on education and inclusion.

5. **Community Foundations and Nonprofits:** Community foundations and nonprofit organizations may offer grants and funding opportunities to support accessibility initiatives in education. Building partnerships with these organizations can help leverage additional resources.

Maximizing Resources:

1. **Grant Writing Assistance:** Utilize grant writing resources and seek assistance from experienced grant writers to maximize success in securing funding. Professional grant writers or grant writing workshops can help ensure that grant applications effectively convey the importance of accessibility initiatives.

2. **Collaborative Partnerships:** Collaborate with other schools, districts, and community organizations to share resources and expertise. Pooling resources through collaborative partnerships can help stretch limited budgets and maximize impact.

3. **In-Kind Donations:** Explore opportunities for in-kind donations of technology equipment, software licenses, and assistive devices. Technology companies, community organizations, and local businesses may be willing to donate resources to support accessibility initiatives.

4. **Volunteer Support:** Engage volunteers from the community, including parents, retirees, and college students, to provide support and assistance with accessibility initiatives. Volunteers can help with tasks such as accessibility assessments, training, and implementation of accommodations.

6. **Professional Development Grants:** Seek professional development grants to support training and capacity-building efforts for educators in the area of accessibility. Grants for workshops, conferences, and certifications can help ensure that teachers have the knowledge and skills to effectively support students with disabilities.

Advocacy for Increased Funding:

1. **Policy Advocacy:** Advocate for policies at the local, state, and federal levels that prioritize funding for accessibility initiatives in education. Join advocacy organizations and participate in advocacy campaigns to raise awareness and influence policy decisions.

2. **Community Engagement:** Engage parents, students, educators, and community members in advocacy efforts to increase funding for accessibility initiatives. Build a coalition of stakeholders who are passionate about ensuring equitable access to education for all students.

3. **Data-Driven Advocacy:** Use data and evidence to demonstrate the impact of accessibility initiatives on student outcomes. Collect and share data on student achievement, graduation rates, and post-secondary success to make the case for increased funding for accessibility.

4. **Partnerships with Legislators:** Build relationships with local legislators and policymakers to advocate for increased funding for accessibility initiatives. Invite legislators to visit schools and see firsthand the impact of accessibility efforts on students with disabilities.

Chapter 21

CASE STUDIES: SUCCESSFUL IMPLEMENTATION OF ACCESSIBILITY

This chapter presents case studies highlighting successful implementation of accessibility initiatives in technology education settings. These case studies offer real-world examples of how schools and districts have prioritized accessibility and made meaningful impacts on the learning experiences of students with disabilities.

Case Study 1: The Tech Academy's Inclusive Curriculum Redesign

Background: The Tech Academy, a high school specializing in technology education, recognized the need to make its curriculum more inclusive for students with disabilities.

Implementation: The school formed a task force consisting of technology educators, special education professionals, and accessibility experts. They conducted a comprehensive review of the existing curriculum, identifying areas where accessibility could be improved.

Outcome: The Tech Academy implemented universal design principles throughout its curriculum, ensuring that all students could access and engage with the material. As a result, students with disabilities reported increased confidence and participation in technology classes, leading to improved academic outcomes.

Case Study 2: District-Wide Assistive Technology Initiative

Background: Smithville School District embarked on a district-wide initiative to enhance accessibility through assistive technology.

Implementation: The district invested in training for teachers and staff on the use of assistive technology tools and resources. They also collaborated with technology companies to secure funding and discounts for assistive technology devices.

Outcome: By integrating assistive technology into classrooms, Smithville School District saw significant improvements in student engagement and achievement. Students with disabilities were able to access the curriculum more effectively, leading to greater academic success and inclusion.

Case Study 3: Virtual Learning Accessibility Initiative

Background: With the shift to virtual learning due to the COVID-19 pandemic, Maplewood High School recognized the need to ensure that online education was accessible to all students, including those with disabilities.

Implementation: The school formed a task force to develop guidelines and best practices for creating accessible online content. They provided training for teachers on accessible design principles and offered technical support for implementing accessibility features in online platforms.

Outcome: As a result of these efforts, Maplewood High School saw a significant increase in student participation and success in virtual learning environments. Students with disabilities were able to fully engage with online coursework, leading to improved academic performance and overall well-being.

Case Study 4: Industry Partnership for Work-Based Learning Opportunities

Background: Riverdale Technical Institute partnered with local technology companies to provide work-based learning opportunities for students with disabilities.

Implementation: The institute collaborated with industry partners to create internship programs tailored to the needs of students with disabilities. They provided accommodations and support to ensure that students could participate fully in the workplace.

Outcome: Through these internships, students gained valuable hands-on experience and developed essential skills for future employment in the technology sector. The program received positive feedback from both students and industry partners, highlighting the impact of collaboration on promoting accessibility and inclusion.

Case Study 5: Community Engagement and Advocacy

Background: Greenfield Middle School launched a community engagement and advocacy initiative to raise awareness about the importance of accessibility in technology education.

Implementation: The school organized workshops and events to educate parents, students, and community members about accessibility issues and solutions. They also worked with local policymakers to advocate for funding and support for accessibility initiatives in schools.

Outcome: Greenfield Middle School's advocacy efforts led to increased community support for accessibility in technology education. The school received grants and donations to invest in assistive technology and professional development for teachers, further enhancing accessibility for students with disabilities.

These case studies demonstrate the diverse approaches that schools and districts have taken to promote accessibility in technology education. By learning from these examples, educators can gain insights and inspiration for implementing their own accessibility initiatives and creating inclusive learning environments for all students.

Chapter 22

PROMOTING ACCESSIBILITY IN ONLINE LEARNING ENVIRONMENTS

As online learning becomes increasingly prevalent, it's paramount to ensure that these platforms are accessible to all students, including those with disabilities. This chapter delves into the unique challenges faced in online learning environments and provides strategies for promoting accessibility.

Understanding Accessibility in Online Learning: Accessibility in online learning encompasses various aspects, including the design of digital content, the functionality of learning platforms, and the usability of communication tools. This section explores the fundamentals of accessibility in online learning and highlights the importance of considering diverse learner needs.

Addressing Technological Barriers: Online learning platforms often present technological barriers that can hinder accessibility for students with disabilities. From compatibility issues with assistive technologies to inaccessible user interfaces, this section discusses common technological challenges and offers solutions for overcoming them.

Designing Accessible Digital Content: Creating accessible digital content is essential for ensuring that all students can engage with course materials effectively. This section provides guidance on designing accessible documents, presentations, videos, and other multimedia resources, along with tools and techniques for making content perceivable, operable, and understandable.

Utilizing Assistive Technologies: Assistive technologies play a crucial role in facilitating access to online learning for students with disabilities. This section explores the various types of assistive technologies available, such as screen readers, speech-to-text software, and alternative input devices, and offers recommendations for integrating these tools into online learning environments.

Ensuring Platform Accessibility: The accessibility of the learning management system (LMS) or online platform used for course delivery is fundamental to the success of students with disabilities. This section examines the accessibility features of popular LMS platforms, as well as best practices for evaluating and selecting accessible platforms that meet the diverse needs of learners.

Providing Alternative Modalities for Engagement: Online learning environments should offer multiple modalities for engaging with course content and participating in activities. This section explores strategies for providing alternative formats, such as transcripts, captions, and tactile materials, to accommodate diverse learning preferences and accessibility needs.

Facilitating Accessible Communication: Effective communication is essential for fostering collaboration and interaction in online learning environments. This section discusses accessible communication strategies, including clear writing practices, synchronous and asynchronous communication options, and inclusive participation norms, to ensure that all students can engage meaningfully.

Training and Supporting Educators: Educators play a crucial role in promoting accessibility in online learning environments. This section explores the importance of providing training and support to educators on accessibility best practices, inclusive teaching strategies, and the use of accessible technology tools, empowering them to create accessible online learning experiences for all students.

Engaging Students in Accessibility Advocacy: Empowering students to advocate for their own accessibility needs is key to promoting inclusivity in online learning. This section discusses strategies for involving students in accessibility advocacy efforts, including providing opportunities for feedback, co-designing accessible learning experiences, and fostering a culture of inclusivity and respect.

Evaluating and Improving Accessibility: Continuous evaluation and improvement are essential for ensuring the ongoing accessibility of online learning environments. This section explores methods for assessing the accessibility of online courses and platforms, collecting feedback from students with disabilities, and implementing iterative improvements to enhance accessibility over time.

Collaborating with Accessibility Experts: Collaboration with accessibility experts, such as disability services professionals and accessibility consultants, can provide valuable insights and support for promoting accessibility in online learning environments. This section discusses strategies for building partnerships with accessibility experts and leveraging their expertise to enhance accessibility initiatives.

Addressing Legal and Compliance Requirements: Legal and compliance requirements, such as the Americans with Disabilities Act (ADA) and Section 508 of the Rehabilitation Act, mandate the accessibility of online learning materials and platforms. This section provides an overview of relevant legislation and discusses implications for online learning design and implementation.

Promoting Awareness and Advocacy: Raising awareness about the importance of accessibility and advocating for inclusive practices is essential for promoting accessibility in online learning environments. This section explores strategies for promoting awareness among stakeholders, including administrators, faculty, students, and the broader community, and fostering a commitment to accessibility at all levels.

Cultivating a Culture of Accessibility: Creating a culture of accessibility requires a collective effort and a commitment to equity and inclusion. This section discusses strategies for cultivating a culture of accessibility within educational institutions, including promoting accessibility policies and practices, celebrating accessibility successes, and fostering a sense of belonging for all learners.

Chapter 23

COLLABORATING WITH INDUSTRY AND TECHNOLOGY COMPANIES

Collaboration with industry and technology companies is a strategic approach to enhancing accessibility in technology education. By forging partnerships with these entities, educational institutions can tap into a wealth of resources, expertise, and real-world applications that enrich the learning experiences of students with disabilities. This chapter delves into the benefits of collaboration, strategies for engagement, and best practices for maximizing the potential of partnerships with industry and technology companies.

The Benefits of Collaboration:

1. Access to Resources: Industry partners often possess cutting-edge technologies, software, and hardware that can be leveraged to enhance accessibility in the classroom. Collaborating with these companies provides access to resources that may otherwise be unavailable to educational institutions.

2. Expertise and Support: Technology companies employ experts in various fields, including accessibility and inclusive design. Collaborating with these professionals enables educators to access specialized knowledge and support in implementing accessibility initiatives.

3. Real-world Applications: Industry collaboration facilitates the integration of real-world applications into technology education. Students benefit from exposure to industry-relevant projects, tools, and workflows, preparing them for future careers in technology.

4. Innovation and Research: Technology companies are at the forefront of innovation and research in accessibility technology. Collaboration with these entities fosters innovation in educational practices and ensures that educators stay abreast of the latest developments in the field.

Strategies for Engagement:

1. Identify Potential Partners: Begin by identifying industry and technology companies with a commitment to accessibility and inclusivity. Research companies that develop assistive technologies, accessibility software, or inclusive design solutions.

2. Establish Clear Objectives: Clearly define the objectives and expectations of the collaboration. Determine how industry partners can contribute to enhancing accessibility in technology education and articulate the mutual benefits of the partnership.

3. Build Relationships: Cultivate relationships with key stakeholders within industry and technology companies. Attend networking events, conferences, and workshops to connect with professionals who share an interest in accessibility and education.

4. Collaborative Projects: Explore opportunities for collaborative projects that benefit both parties. Engage industry partners in curriculum development, guest lectures, or student mentorship programs focused on accessibility and inclusive design.

5. Promote Mutual Learning: Foster a culture of mutual learning and exchange between educators and industry partners. Encourage dialogue, sharing of best practices, and collaborative problem-solving to address challenges in promoting accessibility.

Best Practices for Maximizing Partnerships:

1. Commitment to Accessibility: Ensure that industry partners share a commitment to accessibility and inclusivity. Prioritize collaboration with companies that actively promote accessibility in their products, services, and corporate culture.

2. Sustainability and Long-term Engagement: Aim for sustainable partnerships that extend beyond one-time projects or initiatives. Establish long-term relationships with industry partners based on shared goals, mutual trust, and ongoing collaboration.

3. Inclusive Design Principles: Integrate inclusive design principles into collaborative projects and initiatives. Work with industry partners to develop products, software, and technologies that prioritize accessibility from the outset.

4. Student Engagement and Internships: Facilitate opportunities for student engagement, internships, and experiential learning with industry partners. Encourage students to participate in industry-sponsored projects, internships, or co-op programs focused on accessibility.

5. Evaluation and Feedback: Regularly evaluate the effectiveness of collaborative efforts and solicit feedback from both educators and industry partners. Use feedback to refine collaboration strategies, address challenges, and maximize the impact of partnerships.

Chapter 24

PROMOTING CAREER OPPORTUNITIES FOR STUDENTS WITH DISABILITIES

Technology careers offer a vast array of opportunities for individuals to innovate, create, and contribute to society. However, students with disabilities often face barriers when pursuing career paths in technology-related fields. Promoting career opportunities for these students involves breaking down barriers, fostering inclusivity, and providing the necessary support and resources for success.

Understanding the Landscape: This section provides an overview of the current landscape of career opportunities in technology for individuals with disabilities. It examines trends, challenges, and existing initiatives aimed at promoting diversity and inclusion in the workforce.

Identifying Strengths and Abilities: Every individual, regardless of disability, possesses unique strengths and abilities. This chapter explores strategies for helping students with disabilities identify their strengths and interests, aligning them with potential career paths in technology.

Career Exploration and Exposure: Exposure to various career options is crucial for students with disabilities to make informed decisions about their future.

This chapter discusses the importance of career exploration activities, such as internships, job shadowing, and mentorship programs, in providing students with hands-on experience and exposure to different technology-related careers.

Skill Development and Training: Building a strong foundation of technical skills and competencies is essential for success in technology careers. This section explores strategies for providing students with disabilities with access to high-quality training programs, certifications, and professional development opportunities.

Accessibility in the Workplace: Creating an inclusive workplace environment is vital for ensuring that individuals with disabilities can thrive in their careers. This chapter discusses best practices for promoting accessibility in the workplace, including accommodations, assistive technologies, and supportive policies.

Building Networks and Support Systems: Networking plays a critical role in career advancement. This section explores strategies for helping students with disabilities build professional networks, connect with mentors and peers, and access support systems within the technology industry.

Promoting Entrepreneurship and Innovation: Entrepreneurship offers an alternative pathway for individuals with disabilities to pursue careers in technology. This chapter examines the opportunities and challenges of entrepreneurship for students with disabilities and provides resources and guidance for aspiring entrepreneurs.

Advocacy and Empowerment: Advocacy is essential for promoting systemic change and creating more inclusive opportunities in the technology sector. This section discusses the role of advocacy organizations, government agencies, and grassroots movements in advancing the rights and interests of individuals with disabilities in the workforce.

Success Stories and Role Models: Highlighting success stories and role models can inspire and motivate students with disabilities to pursue careers in technology. This chapter profiles individuals with disabilities who have achieved success in various technology-related fields, showcasing their accomplishments and contributions.

Collaboration with Industry Partners: Collaboration with industry partners is essential for creating pathways to employment for students with disabilities. This section explores strategies for partnering with technology companies, organizations, and employers to create inclusive hiring practices and internship opportunities.

Measuring Success and Impact: Evaluating the effectiveness of career promotion initiatives is crucial for continuous improvement. This chapter discusses methods for measuring success and impact, such as tracking employment outcomes, gathering feedback from stakeholders, and conducting program evaluations.

Chapter 25

ENSURING EQUITABLE ACCESS TO EXTRACURRICULAR TECHNOLOGY ACTIVITIES

Extracurricular technology activities, ranging from robotics clubs to coding competitions, offer invaluable opportunities for students to explore their interests, develop skills, and foster creativity outside the traditional classroom setting. However, ensuring equitable access to these activities for students with disabilities is paramount to promoting inclusivity and fostering a supportive learning environment. This chapter delves into various strategies and considerations for ensuring that all students, regardless of their abilities, can participate fully in extracurricular technology activities.

Understanding the Importance of Extracurricular Technology Activities

Extracurricular technology activities play a crucial role in complementing classroom learning, providing hands-on experiences, and nurturing students' passion for technology and innovation. However, students with disabilities may face barriers that hinder their participation in these activities. Understanding the significance of these activities and their potential impact on students' academic and personal growth underscores the importance of ensuring equitable access

Identifying Barriers to Participation: Before addressing accessibility concerns, it's essential to identify the barriers that students with disabilities may encounter when attempting to participate in extracurricular technology activities. These barriers can be physical, such as inaccessible facilities or equipment, or systemic, such as lack of accommodations or support services. By pinpointing these barriers, educators and administrators can develop targeted strategies to address them effectively.

Creating Inclusive Program Design: Designing extracurricular technology programs with inclusivity in mind is key to ensuring equitable access for all students. This involves considering factors such as physical accessibility, accommodation needs, and diverse learning styles when planning activities and events. By adopting universal design principles, educators can create environments that are welcoming and accessible to students with disabilities from the outset.

Providing Individualized Accommodations and Supports: Recognizing that the needs of students with disabilities vary widely, providing individualized accommodations and supports is essential for facilitating their participation in extracurricular technology activities. This may include providing assistive technology tools, assigning peer mentors or aides, or modifying activities to meet specific needs. By tailoring supports to the unique needs of each student, educators can empower them to engage fully in the activities and achieve success.

Training and Capacity Building: Equipping staff and volunteers with the knowledge and skills to support students with disabilities is integral to ensuring inclusive participation in extracurricular technology activities. Providing training on disability awareness, inclusive practices, and effective communication can help create a supportive environment where all students feel valued and respected. Additionally, fostering a culture of collaboration and teamwork among staff encourages them to work together to address accessibility challenges proactively.

Promoting Peer Support and Collaboration: Peer support and collaboration can play a significant role in promoting inclusivity within extracurricular technology activities. Encouraging peer mentoring, group work, and collaborative problem-solving not only benefits students with disabilities but also fosters empathy, understanding, and camaraderie among all participants. By nurturing a culture of inclusivity and mutual support, educators can create a positive and empowering environment where every student feels included and valued.

Engaging with Community Partners and Resources: Engaging with community partners, such as disability advocacy organizations, technology companies, and local businesses, can provide valuable resources and support for promoting equitable access to extracurricular technology activities. Partnering with these organizations can facilitate access to assistive technology tools, funding opportunities, and expertise in accessibility best practices. By leveraging community resources, educators can enhance the accessibility and quality of extracurricular technology programs for students with disabilities.

Ensuring Continuous Evaluation and Improvement: Continuous evaluation and improvement are essential for ensuring that efforts to promote equitable access to extracurricular technology activities are effective and sustainable. Regularly soliciting feedback from participants, parents, and staff, and incorporating their input into program planning and implementation, allows for ongoing refinement and adjustment. By embracing a culture of continuous learning and improvement, educators can enhance the accessibility and inclusivity of extracurricular technology activities over time.

Chapter 26

PROMOTING ACCESSIBILITY IN STEM EDUCATION

STEM (Science, Technology, Engineering, and Mathematics) education serves as a gateway to numerous opportunities in the modern world. However, ensuring accessibility in STEM education for students with disabilities is paramount to fostering inclusivity and diversity in these fields. This chapter delves into the challenges faced by students with disabilities in STEM education and outlines strategies for promoting accessibility.

Understanding the Challenges: Students with disabilities often encounter barriers in STEM education, ranging from inaccessible classroom materials to a lack of accommodations for hands-on experiments and fieldwork. Additionally, attitudinal barriers and stereotypes can discourage students with disabilities from pursuing STEM subjects.

Adapting Curriculum and Instruction: One approach to promoting accessibility in STEM education is through curriculum and instruction adaptations. This involves modifying lesson plans, materials, and teaching strategies to accommodate diverse learning needs. For example, providing alternative formats for textbooks and incorporating tactile learning materials can benefit students with visual impairments.

Utilizing Assistive Technologies: Assistive technologies play a crucial role in levelling the playing field for students with disabilities in STEM education. From screen readers and speech-to-text software to adaptive lab equipment, these technologies enable students to fully participate in classroom activities and experiments.

Universal Design Principles: Applying universal design principles ensures that STEM learning environments are accessible to all students, regardless of their abilities. Designing labs, experiments, and projects with flexibility and inclusivity in mind can benefit not only students with disabilities but also the entire student body.

Inclusive Pedagogical Practices: Inclusive pedagogical practices promote active engagement and participation among all students. Group work, peer mentoring, and project-based learning foster collaboration and support students with disabilities in developing essential STEM skills.

Teacher Training and Professional Development: Equipping educators with the knowledge and skills to support students with disabilities is essential for promoting accessibility in STEM education. Professional development opportunities should focus on inclusive teaching strategies, assistive technology integration, and creating accessible learning environments.

Collaboration with Special Education Professionals: Collaboration between STEM educators and special education professionals enhances the accessibility of STEM education. Special education teachers can provide valuable insights into the needs of students with disabilities and offer guidance on effective instructional strategies and accommodations.

Advocacy and Policy Initiatives: Advocacy efforts are crucial for promoting accessibility in STEM education at the institutional and policy levels. Educators, administrators, and stakeholders can advocate for inclusive policies, funding for assistive technologies, and resources to support students with disabilities in STEM fields.

Community Engagement and Outreach: Engaging with the broader community promotes awareness and support for accessibility initiatives in STEM education. Partnerships with disability organizations, industry leaders, and STEM professionals can provide valuable resources and mentorship opportunities for students with disabilities.

Research and Evaluation: Research plays a vital role in identifying effective practices for promoting accessibility in STEM education. Evaluating the impact of accessibility initiatives and gathering feedback from students and educators inform continuous improvement efforts.

Chapter 27

ADDRESSING INTERSECTIONALITY IN ACCESSIBILITY INITIATIVES

Recognizing the multifaceted nature of diversity and inclusion, addressing intersectionality in accessibility initiatives is crucial for ensuring that all students, including those with disabilities, receive equitable opportunities in technology education. Intersectionality acknowledges that individuals may experience intersecting forms of discrimination or privilege based on various aspects of their identity, such as race, gender, socioeconomic status, sexual orientation, and disability. In this chapter, we explore how intersectionality intersects with accessibility initiatives and provide strategies for addressing the unique needs of diverse student populations.

Understanding Intersectionality: Intersectionality recognizes that individuals' experiences of oppression and privilege are shaped by the interaction of multiple social identities. For example, a student with a disability who also belongs to a marginalized racial or ethnic group may face compounded barriers in accessing technology education compared to a student with a disability who belongs to a more privileged group. Understanding intersectionality requires acknowledging the complexity of students' identities and experiences.

Identifying Intersecting Forms of Discrimination: In addressing intersectionality in accessibility initiatives, it's essential to recognize and identify intersecting forms of discrimination that students may face. This includes examining how factors such as race, gender, socioeconomic status, sexual orientation, and disability intersect to create unique barriers to access and participation in technology education. By identifying these intersections, educators can better understand the diverse needs of their students and develop targeted strategies to address them.

Tailoring Support and Resources: One-size-fits-all approaches to accessibility may not effectively address the diverse needs of students with intersecting identities. Therefore, it's essential to tailor support and resources to meet the specific needs of different student populations. This may involve providing culturally responsive accommodations, offering mentorship and support networks for marginalized students, and ensuring that educational materials and resources are inclusive and representative of diverse perspectives.

Cultural Competence and Sensitivity: Cultural competence and sensitivity are vital aspects of addressing intersectionality in accessibility initiatives. Educators must be aware of their own biases and privilege and strive to create inclusive learning environments where all students feel valued and respected. This includes incorporating diverse perspectives into the curriculum, fostering open dialogue about social identities and intersectionality, and actively challenging stereotypes and discrimination.

Collaborative Partnerships: Collaborative partnerships with community organizations, advocacy groups, and cultural centres can provide valuable insights and support in addressing intersectionality in accessibility initiatives. By working together with stakeholders from diverse backgrounds, educators can leverage their expertise and resources to develop more comprehensive and effective strategies for promoting inclusivity and accessibility in technology education.

Policy and Advocacy: Advocating for policies and practices that address intersectionality is essential for creating systemic change in accessibility initiatives. This may involve advocating for inclusive hiring practices, equitable allocation of resources, and the integration of intersectional perspectives into educational policies and frameworks. By advocating for systemic change, educators can help create more equitable and inclusive environments for all students.

Chapter 28

LEGISLATION AND POLICIES FOR ACCESSIBILITY IN EDUCATION

Legislation and policies serve as the foundation for ensuring accessibility in education for students with disabilities. This chapter delves into the various laws and regulations at international, national, and local levels that mandate accessibility in technology education and outline the rights of students with disabilities.

International Frameworks for Accessibility: At the international level, several frameworks set standards for accessibility in education. The United Nations Convention on the Rights of Persons with Disabilities (UNCRPD) is a significant document that emphasizes the right to education for individuals with disabilities. It calls for inclusive education and accessible learning materials, including technology resources.

National Legislation and Civil Rights Protections: Many countries have enacted national legislation to protect the rights of individuals with disabilities in education. In the United States, the Individuals with Disabilities Education Act (IDEA) ensures that students with disabilities receive a free and appropriate public education (FAPE), including access to technology education. Additionally, the Americans with Disabilities Act (ADA) prohibits discrimination on the basis of disability and requires that public entities, including schools, provide accessible technology and accommodations.

European Union Directives on Accessibility: In the European Union, directives such as the Web Accessibility Directive and the European Accessibility Act aim to harmonize accessibility standards across member states. These directives require public sector bodies, including educational institutions, to ensure that their digital content and services are accessible to all, including students with disabilities.

Local Policies and Guidelines: Many regions and localities have their own policies and guidelines regarding accessibility in education. These may include specific requirements for technology accessibility in schools, such as the use of accessible learning management systems (LMS) and the provision of assistive technologies.

Case Law and Legal Precedents: Case law and legal precedents also play a crucial role in shaping accessibility in education. Court rulings and legal settlements often clarify the obligations of educational institutions regarding accessibility and may establish precedents for future cases.

Emerging Trends and Evolving Legislation: As technology and educational practices evolve, so too do legislation and policies relate to accessibility. Emerging trends include efforts to address digital accessibility, such as ensuring that online learning platforms and educational websites are accessible to students with disabilities.

Challenges and Compliance Issues: Despite legal protections, challenges remain in ensuring full compliance with accessibility laws and policies. These challenges may include limited resources, lack of awareness or training, and resistance to change. Addressing these challenges requires ongoing advocacy, education, and collaboration among stakeholders.

Enforcement Mechanisms and Accountability: Enforcement mechanisms vary depending on the jurisdiction but often include agencies or offices responsible for monitoring compliance with accessibility laws. These agencies may conduct audits, investigations, and enforcement actions to ensure that educational institutions fulfil their obligations.

Future Directions and Policy Recommendations: Looking ahead, policymakers and advocates continue to push for stronger protections and greater accessibility in education. Future directions may include updates to existing laws, increased funding for accessibility initiatives, and greater emphasis on universal design principles.

Chapter 29

BUILDING PARTNERSHIPS WITH DISABILITY ORGANIZATIONS

Building partnerships with disability organizations is a cornerstone of promoting accessibility in technology education. These organizations offer invaluable expertise, resources, and support that can enhance the inclusivity of educational initiatives. This chapter delves into the strategies and benefits of collaborating with disability organizations to ensure that technology education is accessible to all students.

Understanding Disability Organizations: Begin by providing an overview of different types of disability organizations, such as advocacy groups, service providers, and research institutions. Explain their missions, areas of focus, and the populations they serve.

Benefits of Partnership: Highlight the numerous benefits that partnerships with disability organizations can bring to technology education efforts. These include access to specialized knowledge, resources, funding opportunities, and networking connections.

Identifying Potential Partners: Discuss strategies for identifying and reaching out to disability organizations that align with the goals and needs of your technology education program. This may involve conducting research, attending conferences, or leveraging existing professional networks.

Establishing Collaborative Relationships: Outline best practices for establishing collaborative relationships with disability organizations. Emphasize the importance of communication, mutual respect, and shared goals in fostering effective partnerships.

Areas of Collaboration: Explore various areas in which technology educators can collaborate with disability organizations. This may include curriculum development, professional development training, assistive technology implementation, and advocacy efforts.

Resource Sharing and Capacity Building: Discuss strategies for sharing resources and building the capacity of both technology educators and disability organizations. This may involve providing training workshops, sharing best practices, or co-developing educational materials.

Engaging Stakeholders: Highlight the importance of engaging stakeholders, including students, parents, teachers, administrators, and community members, in partnership initiatives with disability organizations. Emphasize the role that each stakeholder group can play in promoting accessibility and inclusivity.

Addressing Challenges and Barriers: Acknowledge that building partnerships with disability organizations may present challenges, such as logistical barriers, funding constraints, or differing priorities. Discuss strategies for overcoming these challenges through open communication, flexibility, and creative problem-solving.

Sustaining Partnerships: Provide guidance on how to sustain long-term partnerships with disability organizations. This may involve regular communication, evaluation of partnership outcomes, and ongoing collaboration on new initiatives.

Case Studies: Include case studies or examples of successful partnerships between technology educators and disability organizations. Highlight the positive impact that these partnerships have had on enhancing accessibility and inclusivity in technology education.

Chapter 30

RESEARCH AND EVIDENCE-BASED PRACTICES

In the pursuit of promoting accessibility in technology education for students with disabilities, it is imperative to ground practices in research and evidence-based approaches. This chapter delves into key findings from research studies and evidence-based practices that inform effective strategies for creating inclusive learning environments.

6. **Understanding the Needs of Diverse Learners:** Research indicates that students with disabilities have diverse learning needs that require individualized support. Studies by Rose and Meyer (2002) emphasize the importance of Universal Design for Learning (UDL) principles in addressing these needs. UDL suggests providing multiple means of representation, expression, and engagement to accommodate diverse learning styles and abilities.

7. **Impact of Assistive Technologies:** Numerous studies have demonstrated the positive impact of assistive technologies on students' academic performance and engagement. For instance, research by Edyburn (2010) highlights how assistive technologies enhance access to curriculum content and promote independence among students with disabilities.

8. **Inclusive Curriculum Design:** Evidence suggests that inclusive curriculum design positively influences student outcomes. Research by Black-Hawkins et al. (2006) emphasizes the benefits of differentiated instruction and curriculum adaptations in meeting the diverse learning needs of students with disabilities.

9. **Teacher Training and Professional Development:** Studies have shown that effective teacher training and professional development programs significantly impact educators' ability to support students with disabilities. Research by Darling-Hammond et al. (2009) underscores the importance of ongoing, job-embedded professional development that focuses on evidence-based practices in technology education.

10. **Universal Design Principles:** Research on Universal Design principles underscores its effectiveness in creating inclusive learning environments. Studies by Burgstahler (2015) highlight the importance of applying Universal Design principles not only to physical spaces but also to curriculum, instruction, and assessment in technology education.

7. **Accommodations and Modifications:** Evidence suggests that providing appropriate accommodations and modifications positively influences students' academic performance and self-esteem. Research by Scruggs and Mastropieri

(2002) emphasizes the importance of individualized support tailored to students' unique needs and preferences.

8. **Parent and Family Engagement:** Research indicates that parent and family engagement significantly impact students' academic success and well-being. Studies by Jeynes (2007) highlight the importance of building partnerships between educators and families to support students with disabilities effectively.

9. **Assessment and Evaluation:** Evidence-based assessment and evaluation practices are essential for monitoring students' progress and informing instructional decisions. Research by Popham (2009) underscores the importance of using multiple measures and formative assessments to gauge student learning and adjust instruction accordingly.

10. **Impact of Inclusive Classroom Culture:** Research suggests that fostering an inclusive classroom culture contributes to positive academic and social outcomes for all students. Studies by Mertens (2010) emphasize the role of teachers in creating supportive, respectful learning environments where diversity is celebrated and valued.

11. **Intersectionality and Diversity:** Recognizing the intersectionality of students' identities and experiences is essential for promoting equity and inclusion in technology education. Research by Collins (2000) highlights the importance of

addressing multiple dimensions of diversity, including race, ethnicity, gender, and socioeconomic status, in educational settings.

Chapter 31

CONTINUOUS IMPROVEMENT AND REFLECTION

Continuous improvement and reflection are integral components of promoting accessibility in technology education. This chapter delves into the ongoing process of refining practices, learning from experiences, and fostering a culture of growth and inclusivity.

The Cycle of Continuous Improvement: At the heart of continuous improvement is a cyclical process of planning, implementing, assessing, and adjusting. This cycle begins with setting clear goals and objectives for promoting accessibility in technology education. Educators then implement strategies and interventions to meet these goals, closely monitoring their effectiveness through ongoing assessment and evaluation. Based on the results, adjustments are made to improve outcomes and address emerging needs. This iterative process ensures that accessibility initiatives remain responsive to the evolving needs of students with disabilities.

Data-Informed Decision Making: Data serves as a cornerstone for informed decision making in continuous improvement efforts. Educators collect various forms of data, including student performance data, feedback from stakeholders, and assessment results, to gain insights into the effectiveness of accessibility initiatives. Analysing this data allows educators to identify areas of strength and areas for improvement, guiding their decision-making process. By utilizing data-driven approaches, educators can prioritize resources effectively and tailor interventions to meet the diverse needs of students with disabilities.

Reflection and Self-Assessment: Reflection is a powerful tool for professional growth and development. Educators engage in regular reflection to critically examine their practices, beliefs, and biases regarding accessibility in technology education. Through self-assessment, educators identify strengths and areas for growth, reflecting on their successes and challenges in promoting accessibility. This reflective practice fosters a culture of continuous learning and improvement, empowering educators to refine their approaches and enhance their impact on student learning.

Feedback Loops and Stakeholder Engagement: Feedback loops play a crucial role in continuous improvement efforts. Educators seek input from students, parents, colleagues, and other stakeholders to gain diverse perspectives on accessibility initiatives. By soliciting feedback, educators can identify areas of concern, gather insights into student experiences, and collaborate with stakeholders to co-create solutions. Engaging stakeholders in the continuous improvement process fosters ownership and buy-in, ensuring that accessibility initiatives are responsive to the needs of the entire school community.

Professional Learning Communities: Professional learning communities (PLCs) provide valuable opportunities for educators to collaborate, share best practices, and engage in collective problem-solving. Within PLCs, educators come together to discuss challenges related to promoting accessibility in technology education, exchange ideas, and support one another in implementing effective strategies. By participating in PLCs, educators benefit from collective wisdom, peer accountability, and shared responsibility for continuous improvement.

Celebrating Successes and Recognizing Growth: Celebrating successes and recognizing growth is essential for sustaining momentum in continuous improvement efforts. Educators acknowledge and celebrate milestones, achievements, and progress made in promoting accessibility in technology education. By highlighting successes, educators cultivate a culture of positivity and motivation, inspiring continued dedication to accessibility initiatives. Recognizing growth also validates the hard work and commitment of educators, fostering a sense of pride and accomplishment in their efforts to create inclusive learning environments.

Conclusion

In the journey towards inclusive education, the promotion of accessibility in technology education stands as a pivotal point of progress. Throughout this exploration, we have delved into the multifaceted dimensions of accessibility, confronting challenges head-on while embracing a vision of equity and empowerment for all students, regardless of their abilities.

Firstly, we have come to understand that accessibility in technology education extends far beyond physical accommodations. It encompasses a spectrum of considerations, from the design of digital content to the cultivation of inclusive classroom cultures. By recognizing the diverse needs of students with disabilities, we lay the groundwork for meaningful engagement and learning experiences.

In addressing these needs, a myriad of strategies has emerged. From the adoption of assistive technologies to the implementation of universal design principles, educators are equipped with a toolbox of approaches to foster accessibility. Collaboration with special education professionals and the engagement of parents and families serve as pillars of support, reinforcing the interconnectedness of stakeholders in the educational ecosystem.

Yet, as we advocate for accessibility, we confront not only physical barriers but also attitudinal ones. Stereotypes and misconceptions must be challenged, replaced by a collective ethos of acceptance and respect. In cultivating inclusive classroom cultures, we sow the seeds of empathy and understanding, nurturing environments where every student feels valued and capable.

Moreover, we recognize the importance of preparing educators to champion accessibility initiatives. Through training and professional development, teachers are empowered to navigate the complexities of diverse learning needs, fostering environments where all students can thrive. Continuous reflection and improvement serve as guiding principles, ensuring that accessibility remains at the forefront of educational practice.

As we conclude this exploration, we are reminded of the transformative power of accessibility in technology education. It is not merely about accommodating students with disabilities; it is about embracing diversity, celebrating individual strengths, and unlocking the full potential of every learner. By advancing accessibility, we pave the way for a more inclusive and equitable future, where barriers are dismantled, and opportunities abound.

In closing, let us commit to the ongoing pursuit of accessibility in technology education, recognizing it not as an endpoint but as a journey of continual growth and evolution. Together, let us forge a path where every student, regardless of their abilities, can thrive, contribute, and succeed in the ever-expanding landscape of technology and innovation.

www.ingramcontent.com/pod-product-compliance
Lightning Source LLC
Chambersburg PA
CBHW070258230526
45470CB00002B/627